When Universities are Destroyed

When Universities are Destroyed

How Tulane University and the University of Alabama Rebuilt after Disaster

Dr. Jack Kushner

iUniverse, Inc.
New York   Bloomington

When Universities are Destroyed
How Tulane University and the University
of Alabama Rebuilt after Disaster

iUniverse books may be ordered through booksellers or by contacting:

iUniverse
1663 Liberty Drive
Bloomington, IN 47403
www.iuniverse.com
1-800-Authors (1-800-288-4677)

Because of the dynamic nature of the Internet, any Web addresses or links contained in this book
may have changed since publication and may no longer be valid. The views expressed in this work
are solely those of the author and do not necessarily reflect the views of the publisher, and the
publisher hereby disclaims any responsibility for them.

ISBN: 978-1-4502-1100-0 (sc)
ISBN: 978-1-4502-1101-7 (ebook)

Library of Congress Control Number: 2010901526

Printed in the United States of America

iUniverse rev. date: 03/01/2010

Contents

Introduction

When Hurricane Katrina destroyed New Orleans and Tulane University, we at Tulane looked around for a roadmap to assist us in the process of rebuilding. The University of Alabama came to mind, as this institution was also destroyed, though by a military attack and fire during the Civil War, not a hurricane. If roadmap in this case means specific directions on how to rebuild a university, regardless of what destroyed it, then it may not be the correct word to use in the context of this book. But if we use roadmap to suggest examples of how to rebuild an institution after it is faced with disaster, then it is certainly appropriate in describing what this book is about.

Similarly, the word comparison in the context of this book means examining some of the features that are common in the rebuilding of both institutions. Fire destroyed the University of Alabama, and flooding destroyed Tulane University. One cannot compare bricks drenched in muddy flood waters with smoldering bricks covered with soot, but both institutions required large sums of money to rebuild, and both institutions required effective leadership during the rebuilding process. Race was certainly a component in the Civil War, and it played a role in the destruction of the University of Alabama. Although Tulane University has had to deal with racial issues throughout its history, race obviously did not play a role in its destruction. However, race was considered in the rescue efforts and rebuilding of New Orleans. Tulane did establish a committee to deal with race and poverty.

Finally, women sought admission to the University of Alabama, and through the efforts of Julia Tutwiler, women entered the University of Alabama in 1893. In contrast, the women at Newcomb College sought to separate themselves from the men at Tulane University, and even as recently as a few years ago, they attempted through legal means to block the union of Tulane University and Newcomb College. This book is about the destruction of two Southern universities and how each was rebuilt, and the story needs to be told. People should know the history of the University of Alabama, as its football team played in the 2010 Rose Bowl and won the National Championship. For the first time in its history an Alabama football star— Mark Ingram—was awarded the Heisman Trophy

People should also know the history behind Tulane University, as it has just received the largest gift in its history, $50 million, and as it has received many accolades for its role in the rebuilding of New Orleans. Although Tulane cannot boast about its football team, many in New Orleans take pride in the achievements of the New Orleans Saints. Their success means much to the city and its citizens.

Chapter 1

Days Prior to Hurricane Katrina

New Orleans was no stranger to inclement weather, and the threat of flooding there had always been a possibility from the very beginning. In fact, as early as the early 1700s Francois Xavier de Charlevoix, a Jesuit traveler and author of *Histoire de la Nouvelle France*, questioned why Pierre Le Moyne, sieur d'Iberville, and Jean Baptiste Le Moyne, sieur de Bienville, selected the site of New Orleans for a potential city.(3) The location of New Orleans had initially impressed Charlevoix because of its proximity to the Mississippi River, the Gulf of Mexico, Cuba's port of Havana, the Caribbean islands, and the English colonies. Even though the Company of the Indies named New Orleans as the capital of Louisiana on December 23, 1721, Charlevoix did not agree.(3)

Some suggested that Natchez or even Mobile would be better choices for a major city. In his book *Bienville's Dilemma*, Richard Campanela says that Jean Baptiste Le Moyne, sieur de Bienville, based his decision "derived largely from rational and carefully weighted geographical reasons of accessibility, defendability, riverine position, arability, and natural resources, plus a lack of better alternative."(3) In a subsequent letter to Minister Pontchartrain, Bienville expressed some concerns: "The river has been very high for three months and has overflowed in several places above New Orleans. It has destroyed several levees so that more than half of the lands of the inhabitants are submerged."(3)

The importance of the Mississippi River to the growth and development of New Orleans cannot be overstated. The city is connected to the Mississippi River geologically and historically. The river is part of the city's culture, and it is a vital waterway for trade to a large portion of the United States. The crops that have grown in this area are dependent on the Mississippi River, as are the many industries in Louisiana. Scientists have realized for more than one hundred years that the Mississippi River could jump its banks, circumvent New Orleans, and create a huge bay area. In order to prevent this from occurring, the Army Corps of Engineers built the Old River Control Structure between 1954 and 1962(3)

Tulane University can trace its origins back to catastrophic weather. In 1832, there was a shipwreck near Folly Island, near Charleston, South Carolina. Some of the survivors were later treated for cholera. Dr. Thomas Hunt of Charleston felt that a medical school should be established in the South that would specialize in tropical medicine. Due to frequent cholera and yellow fever epidemics, New Orleans had a reputation for being disease-ridden. The Medical College of Louisiana was founded in 1834 and was later renamed Tulane University when Paul Tulane donated a large sum of money. Tulane was a successful businessman from New Jersey, and he had originally considered donating substantial funds to Princeton University, but he ultimately endowed Tulane University instead.

The first medical students entered the Medical College of Louisiana on April 5, 1836, and they did some of their work at the charity hospital, which became part of the University of Louisiana in 1847. An academic wing was built in 1850. Initially, the local residents did not support the university, although the medical school did well. During the Civil War the university was closed for four years, but it reopened in November 1865, and the law school opened at about the same time. The general academic school did not survive during this period. Tulane's first president was William Preston Johnston. The first building on the present campus was built in 1894, and it was named after Senator Randall Lee Gibson, who had persuaded Paul Tulane to endow the university.

Josephine Louise Newcomb founded H. Sophie Newcomb Memorial College in 1886, in honor of her daughter Harriett Sophie Newcomb. This was the first degree-granting college for women established within the framework of a major institution for men.

In 2005, Hurricane Katrina did not come as a surprise to the citizens of New Orleans. In fact, the National Hurricane Center in Miami had been issuing reports on Tropical Depression 12 as early as August 23, when the low-pressure system was still in the Bahamas. Through the years there have been numerous storms and hurricanes in the Gulf region. Indeed, Hurricane Ivan had hit the area in 2004, which resulted in the closing of Tulane University for a few days. The National Weather Service reports on Hurricane Katrina were not initially clear that the hurricane would make landfall at New Orleans. Some weather models predicted that the hurricane could make landfall east of New Orleans in Pensacola, Florida, and others predicted that the hurricane might strike Texas. Others hoped the hurricane would diminish in intensity and revert back to a tropical depression.

The mayor of New Orleans, Ray Nagin, was reluctant to call for a total evacuation of the city. He waited until the last minute because he feared he might be blamed by the hospitality industry and other businesses in New Orleans for unnecessarily diverting business away from their enterprises. (1) But on Saturday August 27, 2005, Tulane President Scott Cowen welcomed the new students to Tulane by saying, "Hello and Good-bye," as he strongly advised all of the students to leave New Orleans immediately.(21) So the sixteen hundred incoming students left New Orleans for various destinations to avoid the approaching hurricane. At least six hundred fifty students and the football team evacuated to Jackson State University in Jackson, Mississippi. Everyone left the uptown Tulane campus except for a few senior administrative personnel, including President Scott Cowen.

Chapter 2

Days Prior to the University of Alabama Attack and Fire

The Congress of the United States donated forty-six thousand acres of land to the territory of Alabama in 1818. Alabama became a state in 1819. The Board of Trustees of the University of Alabama was created in 1821, and students were admitted to the University of Alabama in Tuscaloosa on April 18, 1831. Situated on one thousand acres of land one mile from the city of Tuscaloosa, the university was designed by the state architect William Nichols. Freshmen studied Latin, Greek, geography, English grammar, history, and mathematics. Later, students studied rhetoric, elocution, French, Spanish, or Italian, natural history, botany, natural philosophy, logic, moral philosophy, chemistry, geology, mineralogy, intellectual history, Christianity, and elements of criticism(5)

The first years did not go well for the university. The first president was Alva Woods (1831–1837), who was from New England. He came to Alabama with a Puritan sense of duty and discipline, which was in contrast to the Southern sense of frontier freedom. There were numerous disciplinary problems resulting in suspension of the students from time to time. When President Woods resigned, Reverend Basil

Manly replaced him, serving until 1855. Manly attempted to raise the university's admitting standards. He also tried to create a school to train secondary school teachers, as well as a medical and a law school, but all his efforts failed. The failures stemmed from a lack of discipline and effective leadership. However, Manly was successful in adding an observatory. (20)

The next president was Landon C. Garland (1855–66), who called for and created a military school to inculcate discipline. The Board of Trustees adopted the change to a military school in July 1860. The students wore military uniforms similar to those worn at the U.S. Military Academy at West Point. The atmosphere of the university changed with the uniforms and drilling, and academic performance and class preparation improved.

During the spring of 1865, Major General James Harrison Wilson marched some thirteen thousand five hundred cavalry, infantry, and horse artillery across the Confederate territory. His objective was to stamp out the last vestiges of Confederate resistance. While traveling over five hundred miles, his forces captured five Southern cities and sixty thousand prisoners, and destroyed several factories and arsenals as well as three hundred twenty cannons. Since communication was inadequate, Wilson's men continued to march, destroy, and fight two weeks after General Robert E. Lee surrendered to Lieutenant General Ulysses S. Grant in Appomattox, Virginia, on April 9, 1865.(17)

When Wilson's forces reached the village of Elyton, now Birmingham, Alabama, a side expedition was led by General John T. Croxton of Kentucky. He led eighteen hundred mounted cavalry away from the main body of Wilson's forces and headed toward Tuscaloosa. Although Croxton's men did not meet any Confederate resistance, they did manage to capture a few Confederate soldiers. They did not find much in the way of food since oak and pine trees covered the land, as opposed to farms rich with crops. The people Croxton's men encountered actually thought they were Confederate troops.

Nearing Tuscaloosa, Croxton's forces found that crossing the Warrior River would be a challenge because of the strong current and deep water. Some of the horses and soldiers were swept downstream and drowned. Croxton thought he might encounter Confederate Brigadier General Nathan Bedford Forrest, who was thought to be in the area. Instead, he encountered General Jackson who did not elect to fight as he was looking for General Wilson. Croxton continued on to Tuscaloosa and captured a local man, who warned them that there were about 500 soldiers in Tuscaloosa.

Chapter 3

Summary of Destruction at Tulane University

On August 29, 2005, Hurricane Katrina was bearing down on New Orleans. At 4:30 AM, canal water broke through the floodgates at the Chef Menteur Highway. The tide overwhelmed the levees of the Mississippi River-Gulf Outlet and inundated the residential neighborhoods of the lower Ninth Ward and St. Bernard Parish.(3)

At 6:00 AM: The water flooded the low-lying areas in east New Orleans and the adjacent divisions.

At 6:30 AM: The hurricane hit Barataria Basin, and its eye passed over the towns of Empire and Buras. The Gulf waters rose twenty to thirty feet above normal sea level and flooded the coastal areas of four states. Lake Pontchartrain rose nine feet, the Mississippi River rose sixteen feet, flooding the Plaquemines Parish, and the Industrial Canal rose sixteen feet. The soft marshes under the levees were flooded, and the levees soon failed to function. The first levee failed on the western side of the canal, and this caused the flooding of the Ninth, Eighth, Seventh, and Sixth Wards.

At 7:45 AM: The eastern side of the Industrial Canal failed and more water flooded into the Ninth Ward.

At 8:30 AM: By this time the entire Lower Ninth Ward of Orleans Parish, Arbi, Chalmette, and Mereaux were all submerged and many residents drowned.

At 9:00 AM: The water surged over Orleans Avenue Canal west of City Park.

At 9:45 AM: The Seventeenth Street Canal failed, resulting in the flooding of the Lakeview area.

At 10:30 AM: The London Avenue Canal failed.(3)

Three days later the waters started to recede back into the Gulf of Mexico, and attempts at repairing the levees began.

While the city of New Orleans was being flooded, there were many stories of heroism among the population, and there were many episodes of neglect by the various layers of the government. One of the best documented was written by Dr. David Kline, Chief of Neurosurgery at Louisiana State University Medical School (15)

"The days at Charity hospital were hot and humid following Katrina, and as time passed the air was permeated by a stench that was inescapable. Rendering care to patients without electricity, and thus light and air conditioning, with a temperature in the 90s and no running water was a challenge. Trying to cool patients with central fever and providing adequate ventilation for unconscious patients was extremely difficult. Without elevators, climbs up to and down from the fourteenth floor—where the author and his colleagues had their sleeping rooms—and the twelfth (surgical intensive care unit, seventh neuro ICU, and step-down units), and sixth (medical ICU) floors were tedious. The descent to check the emergency department and obtain a closer look at the flooding in the streets around the hospital, which maintained a four- to five-foot water level, became prohibitive because of the contemplation of the necessary return ascent. There were twenty-one patients, mostly neurosurgical, in the neuro ICU and step-down units and wards."

Hurricane Katrina flooded more than half of Tulane's uptown campus and all of its downtown Health Sciences Center. The hurricane dispersed Tulane's faculty and staff around the world for an entire semester. President Scott Cowen felt that it was his duty to stay and ride the hurricane out after everyone else was safely evacuated. The Reily Student Recreation Center in the Lagniappe Room was established as the command post. Initially after the hurricane came through, Cowen looked out the window and saw tree branches down, telephone and utility wires down, and trash scattered everywhere. The remaining staff spent Monday at the command post and survived the high winds.

By the next morning, the water level was rising. At Willow Street the water was waist high, and in some areas it was eight feet deep. The land phone lines did not work. The cell phones did not work. The only thing that did work was the text messaging system. Cowen felt the vibration of his cell phone in his pocket, but he wasn't sure how to access the text messages. He teamed up with Tony Lorino, a maintenance man who had also stayed throughout the hurricane. They searched all the rooms in several buildings for food, but only located some stale cookies and potato chips. Cowen then learned that Canal Street was covered with nine feet of water and the flooding was headed uptown toward Tulane's upper campus.

On Wednesday morning, Bob Voltz, the electrical superintendent, cut off the electricity in the Reily Center because of the severe flooding. On the previous day, Tony Lorino had noticed two kayaks and an old motorboat under the Reily Center. He and Cowen were able to patch a hole in the boat, craft a steering wheel, and repair the engine. They siphoned gas from a nearby car and then had transportation. They then learned that 80 percent of the campus was under water. Cowen sailed down St. Charles Avenue to the downtown area to find out who was still there and to view the damage.

By the next day, they learned that Bruff Common (university cafeteria) was stocked with food. They found smoked salmon, cheesecake, and ice cream. A mechanic had brought a barbecue smoker from home, which they set up and smoked some hams. Since they had lost their electricity, the Reily Center became insufferably hot, so everyone moved to the roof. Helicopters were hovering nearby. The flight crew thought the staff were refugees and dropped some ready-to-eat meals.

The next day Cowen was evacuated and left for Houston. How did that happen? Anne Banos, the chief of staff, was already in Houston. Although she had no money and each helicopter cost $40,000 to rent, she persuaded the helicopter company to verify her identity with the hotel. After getting clearance for the helicopter from a military base in Omaha, she advised the helicopter company to land at the football field, but it too was covered with water. The first helicopter landed at Memorial Hospital a few miles away, so that was not a working solution. The second one did not arrive and the third one could not see anything but water and returned to its home base. Tracy Boudreaux, a Tulane employee, waded across the Audubon golf course and marked a spot for the helicopter to land using the giant banners that were used for student orientation. So several staff members went by the improvised motorboat, transferred to a dump truck, and made it to the helicopter. From there the group went to

Patterson, Louisiana, boarded a private plane, and flew to Houston.

When the staff met in Houston, several of the administrators gathered in Cowen's hotel room. They had no financial or academic records, or any other type of record showing who was a student and who was a professor at Tulane. Indeed, there was no university at that moment, only a virtual one in their minds. They did not know how they were going to pay their staff or the professors, nor did they know where all of their students were.

The students were effectively placed in five hundred colleges and universities across the country, and an arrangement was made that allowed Tulane University to keep the tuitions paid. The various universities agreed not to charge Tulane or the students for one semester. Other universities agreed not to accept any of the Tulane students for transfer until after they eventually returned to Tulane as a student. Many professors sought refuge at other universities. Although the National Collegiate Athletic Association allowed Tulane athletes to play sports without going to classes for a semester, Athletic Director Rick Dickson insisted that the students attend classes if they were to play sports. Some teams would be at Texas A&M University, Louisiana Tech at Reston, or Texas Tech at Lubbock, and the golf teams would be at Southern Methodist University in Dallas.

The Tulane Emergency Medical Services has two ambulances and all of its members are certified medical technicians. The medical technicians went to Jackson, Mississippi, immediately after the hurricane, and they later went to Baton Rouge. A medical center was established there with an eight hundred–bed facility. This was the largest acute-care field hospital created in U.S. history. They also headed for the New Orleans airport shortly after the hurricane, where they found hundreds of injured patients and no one in charge. They made arrangements to evacuate this group to Baton Rouge.

Although the medical school and hospital had lost power, all of the patients were safely evacuated. The medical students continued their studies at Baylor Medical School, and all graduated on time without losing any time toward graduation. While some in the group started working on recreating the list of students, professors, and university staff workers, others started thinking about acquiring funding to rebuild the university.

President Scott Cowen made three decisions while in Houston: (1) the Tulane uptown campus would reopen in January 2006; (2) the faculty and staff would remain on the payroll as long as Tulane had money; and (3) Tulane would work with other institutions of higher learning to identify academic centers for all Tulane students. With the help of Tulane graduate and Yahoo founder Dave Filo, Cowen sent a message to the Tulane family via a Web site created by Yahoo. Cowen stated that the damage would have to be assessed and decisions would be made, but at the present time water still inundated New Orleans and the streets were blocked. Furthermore, there was no potable water and no electricity, but Tulane would survive just as it had for one hundred seventy-one years. Cowen started thinking about creating the Tulane Renewal Plan.

Meanwhile, Senior Vice President Yvette Jones was in Jackson, Mississippi with some of the evacuated students. All of Tulane's tuition checks were submerged under several feet of water in New Orleans. A former Tulane Alumni Association president, Jenny Kottler, whose husband worked for a national bank, was able to facilitate the exchange of favors with the bank to obtain a bank account with some funding. Jones made a deal whereby Tulane would loan two of its helicopters from the Tulane hospital in exchange for a bank account. Now Tulane had $10 million in a bank account.

Several others worked on obtaining a loan from New York banks. Lehman Brothers was approached, and Harvey Krueger offered to sell bonds on Tulane's behalf, but this was not what Tulane needed. Deutsche Bank loaned money to Tulane for a period of seven years at one point below the London Inter-Bank Offered Rate (the interest rate banks charge each other), and no interest payments would have to be made for the seven-year period.

The administration encouraged Sylvester Johnson, associate vice president of facilities, to make the university habitable within three months. Yvette Jones contacted Balfour, one of the world's largest disaster restoration companies, to start working on the campus as soon as the water receded. Ten days after the hurricane, Johnson arrived on the campus to see that it was still under water, but as the water was receding a noxious mold was left behind. Gibson Hall was cleaned up and was the command post for the National Guard, which guarded the campus along with the police during the cleanup period. Balfour brought with them eight hundred employees. In addition to drying out the buildings, large yellow hoses were used to bring cold, dry air into the buildings to stop the growth of mold. Concentrated efforts were made by this group to retrieve valuable documents from the Amistad Research Center and the Howard-Tilton Memorial Library. In addition, Technical Environmental Services, Inc., was hired to develop a protocol for mold remediation and indoor air quality testing.

Tulane University still had to retrieve all the documents and data that had been safely stored on the fifteenth floor of an office building on Poydras Street. There still was no electrical power in New Orleans and the city was under martial law. Sheriff's deputies escorted the information technology group as they repeatedly climbed fourteen floors and removed fifty boxes as well as computers from the hot, dark building.

It was becoming clear that Hurricane Katrina had engendered expenses of some magnitude for Tulane University. Tulane sustained $200 million in building losses, $50 million of assets were lost, and $150 million of research assets were lost, making a total loss of $650 million.

To retain and attract a faculty, Tulane would have to provide educational facilities and places for the faculty and staff to live. The families needed schools and day care centers, and a transportation system was required. Tulane purchased a $13 million apartment building, and it built additional modular housing units. Tulane leased a twenty-three-thousand-ton Norwegian cruise liner and anchored it on the Mississippi River. The ship could house one thousand people and had facilities for feeding them. In addition, Tulane needed a school especially for the children of the faculty. Lusher School was the closest school to Tulane, and so Tulane offered $1 million if the authorities could ready the school by January for Tulane families and for the children of faculties at other New Orleans educational institutions. The school board agreed to the charter. Tulane offered Dillard University and Xavier University of Louisiana office and classroom space so that students from those schools could take classes from their respective faculties.

Chapter 4

Summary of Destruction at the University of Alabama

A student at the University of Alabama in 1865 provided a firsthand description of General John T. Croxton's attack on the university. This student, J. G. Gowan, says that the University of Alabama was considered the West Point of the Confederacy, although students at the Citadel in Charleston and at the Virginia Military Institute might have had a different point of view. For several days prior to April 1865 there had been rumors that the enemy was approaching Tuscaloosa. Each time these rumors proved to be false. Each time the students had lined up in formation, then broke ranks, and returned to their studies.

Once the students were told that the enemy had reached the Warrior River. When the students went to the river, there were no Union troops. In April the drums beat and the students came to class. The professor immediately surmised that the students were not prepared to recite their lessons. Professor Pratt said, "Now, young gentlemen, I duly appreciate your position; I am aware that you labor under great difficulties, and that your minds have frequently been distracted from your studies by this continuous excitement; but we have the almost positive assurance that all danger has passed, and that there is not now a Yankee in fifty miles of Tuscaloosa. Return to your books, get down to your studies and come prepared for the next recitation."

No one knows whatever happened to that professor, but he was never seen again. He did not know that the Union troops were at that moment within shelling distance of the campus, and that within a few hours the University of Alabama would be attacked and destroyed.

Earlier in the Civil War Alabama students participated in the war effort by serving in the Battle of Chehaw in July 1864, in Macon County, and again in December 1864, in Mobile, Alabama. Many defended the university when the Union soldiers attacked.

The University of Alabama was designated as a military target by Lieutenant General Ulysses Grant as early as 1863, mainly because the university gave to the Confederacy 7 general officers, 25 colonels, 14 lieutenant-colonels, 21 majors, 125 captains, 273 staff and other commissioned officers, 66 non-commissioned officers, and 294 private soldiers. This cadet corps composed of boys attempted to defend the university when attacked.

At around midnight a courier alerted everyone on campus that the Yankees were in town. The long roll of the drums was sounded. Ammunition was distributed. Colonel James T. Murfee was in command of the battalion. The cadet corps deployed into the city, and they went to the site where the old Washington Hall stood at the intersection of Greensboro Street, which led to the river bridge. Colonel Murfee shouted out the command, "Right wheel! Forward march!" Then from somewhere came a response. "Who comes there?" The answer was "Alabama Corps of Cadets." Then someone said, "Let them have it boys!"

The Alabama soldiers fell to the ground and Murfee yelled that he had been shot. After the other Alabama soldiers fired their guns, the enemy ran in the direction of the river. In one hour, the Union soldiers were all over the city, looting stores and shops. Then there was a red glare over the city as the Union soldiers set the buildings on fire. The cadet battalion retreated to the university campus. The cadets were charged with the duty to destroy the ammunition supplies so that the union soldiers would not obtain additional ammunition.

When the cadets finally reassembled about six miles from the university, they could see smoke coming from the burning of the University of Alabama. The one thousand five hundred union soldiers did not come after the three hundred student cadets. So the student cadets marched on to Marion, Alabama, and arrived after three days. People in the city gave them food. Afterward, the cadet corps disbanded and was not to reassemble again.

As the Union troops entered Tuscaloosa, there was some firing, but the Confederate troops quickly left town when they realized they were outnumbered. The union soldiers interrupted a wedding and arrested the bridegroom, who was a captain in the Confederate forces. The females in the party were heard to say, "I do believe it is a sin and a disgrace to the Yankee nation that such proceedings are tolerated."

General Croxton's forces looted and plundered all the buildings in city of Tuscaloosa. Freed slaves were seen walking around with pockets full of Confederate scrip. What they could not just steal, they bought with silver. People kept whatever gold they possessed. The military destroyed a cotton factory, a foundery, two tanneries, and a hat factory. The Union troops destroyed all of the university, except the president's mansion, the Gorgas House, the observatory, and the guardhouse. The reason they did not burn down the president's mansion is that Mrs. Garland, the president's wife, stood in front of their home and refused to let anyone enter. The Washington, Jefferson, Franklin, Johnson, and Lee barracks, the old lyceum, and the mess hall were all burned to the ground.

Chapter 5

Rebuilding Tulane— President Scott Cowen's Renewal Plan

A university is the aggregate wisdom and resilience of its leaders, especially in a crisis, such as the one that arose from Hurricane Katrina. Tulane is fortunate to have such a great team of leaders headed by President Scott Cowen, Senior Vice President Yvette Jones, and Chief of Staff Anne Banos. But the glue that holds this institution together consists of the students and faculty. When Tulane University reopened in January 2006, between 86 and 93 percent of the students returned, having spent the semester, as Tulane was closed, at some other institution. The story of how Tulane University rebuilt after Hurricane Katrina is one to be proud of.(21)

Cowen states that initially while in Houston he just wasn't sure where to start. His wife admonished him to make a list and then start crossing one thing off it at a time as each task was accomplished. Perhaps one of the most important items on the list was the creation and execution of the Tulane Renewal Plan, which had numerous components.

The Plan for Renewal concentrated on reorganizing Tulane into a more efficient university with a forward-thinking vision. A single undergraduate college was created with alterations in the core curriculum to include public service.

(21) Full-time faculty members would henceforth teach undergraduate students, placing the senior faculty in a more visible position. It was necessary to terminate the following departments: mechanical, electrical, and civil engineering, marketing in the Business School, and Sports Management. Several graduate programs were cancelled. The Science and Engineering Department was created anew. Plans were made to renovate eighty-six buildings on the main campus that had sustained considerable water damage.

To create more loyalty to Tulane University instead of to the fraternities and sororities, all freshmen and sophomores would be required to live in the dormitories and study together in residential communities. It is of interest to review some historical aspects of this decision. After World War II, Tulane was by and large a local university. Most of the students were from New Orleans and Louisiana. There were not many dormitories for Tulane men or Newcomb women. So the Greek system of fraternities was welcomed because this provided housing for the increasing number of students who were enrolling from areas outside of New Orleans.(19)

By 1955 more and more out of state students were coming to Tulane, and between 1955 and 1960 almost 50 percent of the men were in fraternities. The fraternities gradually took over the leadership positions on campus, and in time tension arose between the academic components and the fraternity men. The students developed more loyalty to the fraternities than to the university itself, and the neighbors complained of drunkenness, noise, and rowdy behavior. More importantly, the fraternities were a distraction from academic pursuits. However, since the beginning of integration at Tulane, the number of men participating in fraternities has decreased to 40 percent of the student population.(21)

To rebuild New Orleans and Tulane University, all students would participate in community service through the auspices of the Center for Public Service. The Renewal Plan called for the School of Architecture to get involved in designing homes that would be appropriate for the rebuilding of New Orleans and the Gulf Coast. The Partnership for the Transformation of Urban Communities and the Institute for the Study of Race and Poverty were created in association with Dillard, Loyola, and Xavier universities.

It is important to digress and review the history of Tulane University and the desegregation issue, especially in view of the racial situation since the beginning of the United States and particularly the South. This issue was brought to the forefront by charges of discrimination and neglect of the black population in New Orleans during and after Hurricane Katrina. Many felt that if the white population had stayed behind and did not evacuate, the federal government would have made more of an effort to rescue them from the rooftops of houses, the Superdome, and the Convention Center.

On April 12, 1954, shortly before the Supreme Court decision of *Brown v. Board of Education of Topeka, Kansas,* Professor James K. Feibleman, chairman of the graduate school, called a meeting to discuss desegregation at Tulane University.(10) At that meeting the Dean of the College of Arts and Science proposed a resolution that would enable Tulane to admit qualified African American students. This resolution was passed unanimously and sent on to President Rufus Harris.

On May 17, 1954, the Supreme Court rendered their historic decision, which resulted in some demonstrations throughout the South. The Tulane Board of Administrators were divided on this issue, as there were limitations in the gifts of Paul Tulane and Mrs. Newcomb, the charter of the university, and Act 43 of 1884 which said that only white students could attend Tulane University. So, how could the board protect the previous gifts to Tulane and yet comply with the changing social times in the United States? This was no small problem.

On April 12, 1961, the administrators of the Tulane Educational Fund announced that they would admit qualified African American students if it were legally permissible. In the meantime, Mrs. Pearlie Hardin Elloie applied for admission to the School of Social Work, and Miss Barbara Marie Guillory applied for admission to the graduate school. These applications were reviewed by the authorities, and the deans of the respective schools notified the applicants that they were found to be acceptable, *but* it was not legally permissible for Tulane to admit them.

In September 1961, John Nelson, the attorney for the two students, filed suit against Tulane University, and the board hired John Pat Little and Wood Brown to defend the university. Nelson and his legal representative argued that Tulane had received property from the University of Louisiana, had been given special tax considerations by the state of Louisiana, and had the governor of Louisiana, the mayor of New Orleans, and the state superintendent of education as ex officio members of the board. Tulane had also received federal funds in the past. Therefore, they argued, Tulane University was a state agency and was under the jurisdiction of the Fourteenth Amendment of the U.S. Constitution, which prohibits discrimination based on race by state or federal agencies.

The judge issued an opinion that said no school or college could ever escape being under the jurisdiction of the

Fourteenth Amendment. The appeal was made to the Circuit Court of Appeals for the District of Columbia, which ruled on December 5, 1962, saying that Tulane University could not be compelled to admit African Americans. Within about a week, Tulane University had voluntarily admitted African American students. Security at Tulane was increased, but there were no disturbances and Tulane was peaceably integrated.

The Scott S. Cowen Institute for Public Education would endeavor to create programs to improve the education in the public schools of New Orleans. The School of Public Health and Tropical Medicine, founded in 1967, would expand its scope and influence to improve the community health and the environmental health of New Orleans and its surrounding areas. The Tulane Law School would now have the additional responsibility of concentrating on urban relief, disaster rebuilding, and aiding an indigent population. The university would no longer grant degrees in some areas, and eight of the sixteen sports would be temporarily suspended. As a result of discontinuing some departments and some degrees, it was necessary to terminate some professors, some of whom were tenured. This action has resulted in the possibility of censure from the Association of University Professors, but the Tulane faculty has supported the administration in this action.

URBAN build is a social experiment that has its roots in New Orleans. The School of Architecture had spent its semester at Arizona State University, which influenced the faculty and students to consider designing affordable homes that would work from an economic aspect. With this program, the students would design homes suited for the New Orleans area and then work as the contractors and laborers in conjunction with the Neighborhood Housing Services of New Orleans, Inc. The first house took sixteen weeks to build and cost $109,000 to construct; it sold for $125,000. In addition, environmental sociology has attracted students to work with the Green Project, while other students work with the Chartwell Center, which helps children with autism. The Newcomb Institute teaches women how to tear down a ruined house, install drywall, and hang doors, as well as other construction skills.

In the Tulane University Renaissance book there is a quotation. "History will record that once upon a time in a magical city, a proud university stared at the face of death and did not blink. History will record that Tulane University led that magical city to its own recovery and renewal, both of them stronger and more essential than before."(21)

One action the Tulane Board of Administrators approved deserves further attention because of its historical background and the controversy surrounding it. Josephine Louise Newcomb founded H. Sophie Newcomb Memorial College in 1886 in honor of her daughter. Harriett Sophie Newcomb was the first degree-granting coordinate college for women established within the framework of a major university for men. Initially Josephine Newcomb selected the Tulane Board of Administrators to oversee this newly established college. There are several examples of similar arrangements, such as Harvard University and Radcliffe College, and Columbia University with Barnard College.

The initial arrangement called for a separate president and faculty, and the courses offered would be separate and distinct. This relationship has been strained from the beginning, as the leaders at Newcomb College jealously guarded their independence and their individuality. They have always been concerned that the larger Tulane University would swallow them up. With each school having its own administration, the costs were double. In 1957, Tulane offered a plan for combining these schools, but the women at Newcomb were alarmed and rejected the plans. There were combined programs during the 1970s and the 1980s. A single curriculum was adopted in 1979.

In July 1986, a new organization called the Friends of Newcomb's Future was disturbed by what it perceived as a diminution of Newcomb's identity. The organization had the following complaints: (1) the Music Department's role in scheduling space at Dixon Hall; (2) the relocation of some academic departments outside of Newcomb Hall; and (3) the shift of dormitories from all-women dorms to coed dormitories. Then, in 1985, the University Senate adopted a single Code of Conduct for all male and female undergraduates. In addition, the admissions departments of Tulane and Newcomb were combined.

While some saw these modifications as a blow to Newcomb's individuality, others perceived the changes as an effective economic alteration. The number of students applying to Newcomb was decreasing. In 1987, Newcomb College and the College of Arts and Sciences would have a single faculty of Liberal Arts and Sciences, common academic and honor code requirements, and a single promotion and tenure process presided over by a single department.(19) The Department of Art and Music would be known as the Newcomb Department of Art and the Newcomb Department of Music. Two million dollars of Tulane University funds were dedicated to a Newcomb Foundation.

After Hurricane Katrina, Tulane's board voted to combine the two schools and to rename the undergraduate department the Newcomb-Tulane College. Also, the Sophie

Newcomb Memorial College Institute was established as an academic center to enhance women's college experience and education. Although this has resulted in two court hearings, the judges ruled that Tulane University acted in a responsible and legal manner to save the university after the destruction by Hurricane Katrina.

Under President Scott Cowen's leadership, all but a few of the buildings have been repaired and rebuilt. The Alumni House, McAlister Auditorium, and the Social Work building are still being worked on as of this writing. In 2008, over forty thousand applicants applied for admission to the undergraduate school, which has fifteen hundred spaces. This was the largest one-year increase in first-time freshmen in history. This was a seminal event and an important indicator of Tulane's recovery and continued appeal as one of the nation's top universities.

By January 2008, Tulane had repaid all but $100 million of the debt it incurred as a result of the hurricane. Tulane took the unusual step of acquiring a K–12 school, as it needed to have a school for the children of Tulane's faculty. Mayor Ray Nagin of New Orleans appointed President Scott Cowen to chair the city's Bring New Orleans Back Commission, and charged him with the task of reforming and rebuilding the city's failing school system. Tulane has created an Institute for Public Education Initiatives to support the transformation of public education in New Orleans.

On October 16, 2009, Cowen was able to report that he met with President Obama at a town hall meeting in New Orleans, along with a small group of local leaders. President Obama remarked that the improvement in New Orleans' public educational system is probably the most dramatic he has seen anywhere in the country. Education Secretary

Arne Duncan shared this view. He and Cowen visited the John McDonogh High School to engage students in a discussion of the transformation of public education. Then they accompanied Melody Barnes, director of the president's Domestic Policy Council, and Lieutenant Governor Mitch Landrieu on a visit to Café Reconcile, which provides youth from at-risk communities with the experience and interpersonal skills for a successful career in the hospitality and restaurant industries. Tulane University has been recognized as an institution devoted to civic engagement and social entrepreneurship, of which Café Reconcile is a prime example.

Cowen also serves as Commissioner of the New Orleans Redevelopment Authority, which plays a major role in the rebuilding of Orleans Parish in the aftermath of Hurricane Katrina.

On Valentine's Day 2006, Tulane was the first hospital to reopen in downtown New Orleans after more than $90 million in repairs. Inasmuch as Tulane was originally founded as a medical college, it is only appropriate that we spend a little more time discussing some of the medically related problems that resulted from Hurricane Katrina. Some of the groundbreaking research of the world's oldest racial study of risk factors for heart disease in children and young adults was lost when frozen urine and blood samples thawed out. The samples had been collected since 1973. Fortunately, Dr. Gerald Berenson had already analyzed much of the data and saved it on his computer. Research on cancer, AIDS, heart disease, and other ailments was also lost. More than 150 projects at Tulane were lost. One potential disaster was averted. Medical teams were able to break into the university's "hot labs" to destroy some of the world's most dangerous germs used for research. The Tulane Community Health Center at Covenant House provided free care for more than seventy-eight hundred patients. The Latino Health Outreach Project provided free health care for up to fifty people every day.

During the past four years, Tulane has worked diligently into full recovery from the losses incurred as a result of Hurricane Katrina and the subsequent levee failures. Tulane has raised nearly $85 million against its goal of $75 million in private gifts and grants. To date, Tulane has surpassed the $700 million goal and the endowment exceeds $1 billion. The income from the endowment is strengthening the academic core and expediting the financial recovery. Despite the financial problems, Tulane gave out $70 million in scholarships in 2007, and $80 million in scholarships in 2008.

Tulane has every reason to be optimistic about the future, and the sources of this optimism are as follows: Both the student interest and student quality in Tulane have increased; there were thirty-five thousand applicants for fourteen hundred undergraduate spaces in 2007, and forty thousand applicants for these spaces in 2008. The acceptance rate has now been increased to sixteen hundred spaces for the undergraduate college; there were ten thousand applicants for the medical school in 2008, and Tulane accepts one hundred seventy-five students; recruiting faculty and senior level management has been very successful.

Tulane does still have some concerns, as the university is out of pocket $250 million and still owes $100 million, and the operating losses are predicted to persist for a few more years. Tulane needs more investment funds, and it hopes to retain its senior staff. However, Tulane's commitment and dedication to New Orleans and the State of Louisiana are unwavering, and together they will steer a course to a brighter and prouder future.

Tulane has to continue to grow and to renovate. In May 2009, the campus lighting improvements project that extends from Freret Street to Willow Street was started. It was completed in September 2009. This project not only enhances the safety of the students, but also adds to the beautification of the campus. In the summer of 2009, Tulane purchased property on Claiborne Street. The Claiborne substation provides security at that end of the campus, and the Tulane Emergency Medical Services and the Tulane University Police Department will both use it.

The Dinwiddie Hall renovation is in progress, and when completed the hall will house the Anthropology Department, the Middle American Research Institute, and some classrooms. Hopefully, this will be completed in July 2010. In May 2009, the McAlister Place Project was started, which is part of a long-term beautification project that will create a safer and more pedestrian-oriented campus. The demolition of the Anthropology Building was required by FEMA in the fall of 2009. The occupants of the Temporary Building Complex have been relocated. Tulane is removing the decking, roofing, and trailers. There is site grading and pile driving occurring, and this should be completed by January 2010. The Alumni House Renovation continues. The Newcomb Place Drainage is a three-phase project (2009–2010) that will precede the Residential College II construction. The Development of Residential College II involves the conversion of the old Doris site to a Residential College II. Tulane is renovating the Howard-Tilton Memorial Library and the former PIKE house, which the Tulane University Police will occupy.

Chapter 6

Rebuilding the University of Alabama

Immediately after the Civil War, the president of the University of Alabama was Landon C. Garland, who thought that the university should be opened for business on Oct 1, 1866. Although there were no dormitories for the students, he thought some students could stay at the president's mansion, and others could stay with residents in the city of Tuscaloosa. Since the university was on a shoestring budget, he hoped to teach mathematics, Professor Mallet would teach chemistry, Professor Wyman would teach Latin and Greek, and Professor Pratt would teach logic, rhetoric, and oratory.

The only student who appeared on the opening date was the son of ex-Governor Thomas H. Watts of Montgomery. In addition, Professor Pratt had moved to New York, and Professor Mallet was at the medical college of Louisiana, now called Tulane University. The executive committee decided that they could not open the university and attract students until they had more buildings and more faculty. They retained Professor Garland as the president, and charged him with the responsibility of making plans for new buildings and obtaining estimates for this construction. Govenor Parsons and the executive committee asked Garland to put the plans out for bid with several construction companies, hire some workmen, and buy a steam engine and a sawmill for the campus.

Furthermore, he was asked to buy some books for the library and to acquire the necessary instruments for the laboratories. They agreed to pay Garland a salary of $3,000 and to pay the teachers $2,000. Funding for these expenditures would come from the state treasury, with the approval of the governor. The superintendent of the state would also be the treasurer of the university. Finally, Garland was encouraged to send a bill to the Congress of the United States for indemnification for the losses sustained when General Croxton's soldiers destroyed the university.

In a discussion with Dr. Clark E. Center, Jr., university archivist and curator of Southern History and Life, the financial situation at the University of Alabama at the end of the Civil War was illuminated. The treasurer of the University of Alabama was also the bookkeeper, and a banker in Tuscaloosa was the fiscal agent. Confederate dollars were kept in a local bank, and when General Robert E. Lee surrendered at Appomattox, Virginia in April 1865, those Confederate dollars were of no value. The university was broke. However, most of the records of the university were saved. They may have been stored at the mansion of the president or in a building that was spared. A large portion of the records were located in the 1950s in the Round House or the Guard House, which was also called Jason's Shrine and was next to the Gorgas House.

The Alabama General Assembly voted to give the University of Alabama a loan of $70,000 for the purpose of rebuilding the university. A third of the sum could be drawn in 1867, the next third in 1868, and the remainder in 1869. The following people were named to the building committee:

Colonel R. Jemison, Jr., Judge P. King, W. S. Mudd, and J. H. Fitts. However, by the spring of 1867, the Alabama General Assembly concluded that the University of Alabama could not even pay interest on the loan fund. The trustees voted to borrow $7,000 so that the construction could proceed with the acquisition of one million bricks. This loan was negotiated with R. & J. McLester of Tuscaloosa, who in turn agreed to advance $2,000 to the committee.

Dr. Garland then reported that he was having difficulty obtaining timber for the burning of the bricks, as the timber on the university land had been stolen. The projected date for the reopening of the university was pushed up to the fall of 1867. Probably because of Alabama politics, Garland suddenly resigned as president of the university.

Although no new president was named at that time, the fiscal matters were handed over to J. H., Fritts & Co. Colonel James T. Murfee was chosen as the architect, and a contract for the actual building was awarded to G. M. Figh & Co., of Montgomery, which agreed to build what is now Alva Woods Hall for $63,367 by January 1, 1868. This date was too optimistic, as the builders did not start until April 12, 1868, and by that time the supply of bricks had diminished. They learned that they could not salvage the old bricks because they were too damaged, and the saw at the sawmill was not working. Even at that time, by April 1868, the amount already spent was $54,614, which amounted to a $22,000 overrun. Even so, the building was completed by July 1868. This building could accommodate 180 students, and the kitchen could feed five hundred students.

The trustees at the university started selecting a faculty, and they also discussed reorganization and governance plans.

They selected Dr. Henry Tutwiler as the president, and they persuaded Professor Wyman and Dr. Garland to return, along with J. T. Murfee and John Forney. This faculty did not get very far, as the Alabama General Assembly had different ideas.

On November 5, 1867, a state convention assembled in Montgomery and wrote a new state constitution. The government of the University of Alabama was removed from the control of the board of trustees and entrusted to a new board of regents of the state university, which was chosen and controlled by the Alabama Legislature. This board of regents assumed the power to elect a president, appoint the faculty, and make university positions patronage favors. The results were untenable. The *Montgomery Mail* described the board of regents as a group of four scalawags and carpetbaggers. After this group convened in August 1868, they cancelled everything done by the Alabama Board of Trustees, including all accomplishments.

To understand what was happening at the State of Alabama's government level, reference is made to *Black Power in Old Alabama*.(11) The author points out that James Rapier was one of Alabama's most militant congressmen for human rights. In addition to being one of Alabama's first labor organizers, he was also a fiery newspaper editor. He was involved in the resistance to slavery, and after the Civil War he was against all efforts to re-enslave people. He fought against secession and supported underground activity against the Confederate military. He spent most of his public life fighting against the idea that the black man was subhuman and only fit for menial labor for the superior whites.

Rapier was a delegate to the constitutional convention in Montgomery in 1867 that composed and passed the new constitution for the State of Alabama. From this group, he was selected as a delegate to the U.S. Congress. He gave an important oration in Montgomery that celebrated the passage of the Fifteenth Amendment to the Constitution, which was never enforced. He was able to form an alliance between the black population and the whites who never supported secession or the Confederacy. This was the Alabama Republican party, which is different from the present day Republican Party.

After the Civil War, President Andrew Johnson tried to establish white governments in all the Southern states, but the U.S. Congress prevented those attempts. Instead it supported efforts to grant universal suffrage to all, public education for all, and freedom of speech for all, and it encouraged industry to move to the South. These efforts lasted about ten years.

It was due to Rapier's efforts that the new Alabama constitution included a clause on universal manhood suffrage. Rapier was also responsible for inserting a right-to-vote amendment in the federal constitution. Rapier organized a huge parade that went up Dexter Avenue in Montgomery to the capital steps, as he now was secretary of the Alabama Equal Rights Organization. He was the main speaker and publicly thanked U.S. Representative Thaddeus Stevens and Senator Charles Sumner.

Rapier criticized the framers of the 1865 constitution, which made an attempt to enslave the freed slaves by means of restrictive laws called the Black Codes. He realized that they would not achieve freedom unless they had jobs and economic improvement. He called for a convention of the National Labor Union and became vice president of the organization. One proposal that was made but not carried out was to transfer all black people from Alabama to Kansas, but Congress did not approve of this suggestion. By the time Rapier was appointed Collector of the Internal Revenue in 1878, reconstruction was over and the white supremacists were in charge.

After the Civil War, the most visible change was the expansion of American political rights to include African Americans. Now they had the right to own property, marry, and serve on juries under the Fourteenth Amendment. The Fifteenth Amendment gave them the right to vote. By the end of Reconstruction in 1877, sixteen African Americans had served in Congress, and over six hundred served in state legislatures. All these gains were illusory, as Southern whites successfully nullified many of these gains by passing a series of laws later known as the Black Codes. Under these laws African Americans had to sign work contracts each year to farm cotton at low wages, and if they quit work they could be arrested for vagrancy. They lost the right to serve on juries and could not insult whites. The Ku Klux Klan was formed in 1860 and was successful in reducing the status of African Americans to that of second-class citizens.(2)

After the Civil War, the necessity for widespread education was gaining in the minds of Americans. Ever since the founding of the country, education was high on the priority list of white Americans, with an emphasis on reading, writing, and mathematics. Formal education for young children became the norm after 1870 as schools were established in most all of the states. It was widely accepted that publicly supported schools would produce equality among the students and produce future workers, which would sustain economic growth.

In 1862 during the height of the Civil War, Congress passed the Morrill Land Grant Act, which gave each of the states land to support colleges that taught practical and academic studies. This Act enabled states to create new agricultural colleges and institutes of technology. By 1870 there were five hundred colleges and universities throughout the United States, more than in all of Europe. About fifty thousand students attended these colleges, which represented only 1 percent of the college-age population. Only about one quarter of the students were women, and many of these women attended newly created women's colleges, such as Vassar College, which was established in 1865. Wellesley and Smith colleges opened ten years later. Some colleges opened their doors to women, such as Boston University and Cornell. Oberlin, Antioch, and Swarthmore had already functioned for some time as coeducational institutions.(16)

The Alabama Board of Regents wanted to nominate Reverend R. D. Harper and the Reverend A. S. Lakin, both Northerners, for the presidency of the University of Alabama. Harper had been active with the Freedman's Bureau, and Lakin was actively recruiting Alabama African Americans into Loyal Leagues. A native Alabamian nominated Professor Wyman, who won because the other two candidates split their votes and did not get a majority. The board agreed to retain General Forney as professor of modern languages, and H. S. Whitfield as the chairman of rhetoric and oratory.

However, the board wanted to include three men from Ohio for other positions, which caused Wyman and Forney to refuse to serve in any capacity. The Alabama Board of Regents then replaced these men with Reverend A. S. Lakin, Jasper Callans of DeKalb County, and Joseph Kimball of Ohio, granting them professorial chairs. When President Elect Lakin arrived in Tuscaloosa for the keys, Dr. Wyman refused to give them to him or anyone who recognized Lakin as the president. This controversy was publicized by Ryland Randolph, editor of the *Monitor* and one of the first members from Alabama in the Ku Klux Klan. Randolph said, "If these scoundrels expect to live quietly here and draw their salaries, extorted from the sweating brows of the toiling taxpayer of Alabama, we tell them they are mistaken. This community will be too disagreeable for them, and the sooner they resign, the better."(20)

In addition, when Lakin and N. B. Cloud, another Board of Regent appointee, arrived in Tuscaloosa a little later, they noticed a cartoon in the *Monitor*. The cartoon showed two figures hanging from a tree, and one of them was labeled a carpetbagger from Ohio. There was some text under the cartoon which said: "Southern society—the carpetbagger and the scalawag—if found in Dixie's land after the break of day on the 4th of March next—The contract for hanging will be given to the Negro who, having mounted the carpetbagger and the scalawag on the mule that he didn't draw from under them, over the forty acres of ground that he also didn't get, will leave the vagabonds in the air."

Lakin and Cloud left town. The Alabama Board of Regents then sent Reverend R. D. Harper, but Randolph wrote that he would be no more welcome than the others. The board appointed more professors, but all of them left Tuscaloosa soon after their arrival. In addition, the steamboat *Jennie Rogers* arrived in Tuscaloosa carrying furniture for two newly arrived professors. The letters KKK appeared on each article of furniture when the boat docked. Randolph ridiculed all of the Northern professors as they arrived in Tuscaloosa. Reverend Harper resigned and Professor J. De Forest took over as acting president.

On April 5, 1869, the university reopened and had twenty students. N. R. Chambliss served as president for the remainder of the year (1868–69). Additional newspapers continued to harass professors appointed by the Alabama Board of Regents and suggested that they open a school for the freed slaves instead of educating the sons of white Alabamians. The Republican press fought back and said that a university should not exist if it was headed and controlled by the defeated enemy.

Finally, it became obvious that the climate at the University of Alabama was not conducive to academic pursuits. Commodore Mathew Fontaine Maury, formerly of the Union and then Confederate navies, was selected as president of the University of Alabama. He resigned after a short period out of frustration in dealing with the Alabama Board of Regents. Professor Nathaniel Thomas Lupton was then elected president of the university when it opened October 4, 1871, when the atmosphere had improved. He was the first of eight presidents who served the University of Alabama from 1871 to the turn of the century.

Financial matters preoccupied the leaders of the University of Alabama, as there was little hope of obtaining funding from the Alabama State Legislature. For a while there was hope that perhaps Congress could be persuaded to give the University of Alabama the funding that was to be allocated for the agricultural college in an arrangement similar to what the governor of Georgia was able to accomplish. The city of Auburn, Alabama, was able to offer land and buildings from the East Alabama Male College, which had been a Methodist school. Then the University of Alabama tried to persuade Congress to pay for the damages done to the university by the federal troops in 1865, but this effort also failed.

In 1874, the board elected Dr. Carlos Smith as the new president of the university. There were one hundred seventy-nine students by 1878. After the Union troops left Alabama, the state legislature took the governance away from the board of regents and returned it to the board of trustees at the University of Alabama. The board of trustees at the University of Alabama now consisted of the following men: W. G. Clark, H. A. Herbert, John A. Foster, Marion Banks, James Crook, and Edward C. Betts. This new board of trustees created the following committees: finance, university property, salaries and fees, instruction, rules and regulations, and quartermaster. Other committees were added later. These included the executive, judiciary, and education. Two years later, the board invited General Josiah Gorgas to serve as president of the university, which caused a great deal of controversy throughout the state, but members of the board insisted they were not satisfied with the manner Smith handled the finances and that he had to be replaced.

General Gorgas was a West Point graduate who resigned his commission in the Union Army to serve with the Confederate forces. After the war, he managed the iron works in Birmingham and later was the vice chancellor at the University of the South in Sewanee, Tennessee. At the beginning of his second term, he fell ill and was replaced by Boykin Lewis. It is of interest that his son, William Crawford Gorgas, worked with Walter Reed years later in trying to eradicate yellow fever and malaria in the Caribbean and in Panama. General Gorgas died on May 15, 1883.

Lewis was born in Montgomery, Alabama, in 1837. He had been a student at the University of Alabama and later practiced law in Montevallo. He married Rose Garland, the daughter of the respected university president. During his six-year term, the University of Alabama did well, as the state legislature voted a grant of $50,000 and the U.S. Congress gifted land grants to the university. In April 1884, Congress granted 46,080 acres of public lands to the University of Alabama in "An Act to Increase the Endowment of the University of Alabama from the public land in the said State." The Act specifically said that the revenue from the sale of those lands should be used for new buildings at the University of Alabama and for the restoration of the library and scientific apparatus, which had been destroyed by the fire in 1865.(20)

The university procured some thirty thousand acres of land in the Warrior and Cahaba coalfields in the counties of Walker, Jefferson, Shelby, Bibb, and Tuscaloosa. The lands were to be sold and the revenues would revert to the University of Alabama endowment. The receipts for the sale of the land and timber and for rents and royalties totaled more than $200,000, and enabled the university to build Garland, Tuomey, and Barnard halls, as well as to make improvements. In 1884, the board accepted the building plan proposed by William A. Freret of New Orleans.

A review of the buildings at the University of Alabama reveals the stages of construction. On April 4, 1865, the University of Alabama consisted of the following:

Home of Professor and Mrs. Richardson
The Hotel, now known as the Gorgas House
Home of Professor Wyman
President's mansion
Faculty residence
The Observatory
The Guardhouse

The first building completed after the Civil War was originally called the Centre Building, later the barracks, and finally in 1884 it was named after the first president, Alva Woods. Woods Hall was initially drawn up by Commandant James T. Murfee based on Alexander Jackson Davis's plan for the Virginia Military Institute.

In 1883, William A. Freret, a prominent New Orleans architect, planned three buildings to complete the enclosed courtyard plan originated by Murfee in 1868.

Clark Hall built in 1884 and 1885 and Manly Hall in 1885 at a cost of $70,059.73.

Garland Hall, 1888, $22,550

Tuomey Hall, May 1888, $10,150

Barnard Hall, 1889, $9574

Additional faculty houses were built at this time as well:

Little Hall, 1892

Smith Hall, 1910

Comer Hall, 1910

Morgan Hall, 1911

Tutwiler Hall, 1914

Phi Gamma Delta, 1914

Nott Hall, 1922 (university's two-year medical program)

Amelia Gorgas Memorial, 1925

When the school reopened in 1871, there were eleven independent schools, which were reorganized into The Academic Department. Emphasis was placed on a classical education, along with philosophy, mathematics, and science. The University of Alabama was able to attract professors with advanced graduate degrees from Johns Hopkins, Harvard, Heidelberg, and Princeton. By 1872 the following degrees were offered: Bachelor of Arts, Bachelor of Philosophy,

Bachelor of Science, Bachelor of Letters, Civil Engineer, and Master of Arts.

By 1886 the trustees combined the positions of the president of the university with that of the chancellor of the law faculty. In 1907, the Medical College merged with the University of Alabama.

By 1887 the library had twelve hundred volumes. In 1889, a full-time librarian was hired. By 1896 Professor Wyman devised a card catalogue for the fifteen thousand volumes that the university had acquired. General Gorgas and his wife, Amelia Gayle Gorgas, contributed a great deal to the library.

The professors at the University of Alabama insisted on rigorous scholastic standards, and by 1872, they had mandated that incoming students must pass the following examinations:

1. English, covering grammar, geography, and Hart's *First Lessons in Composition*;

2. Latin grammar, including prosody; Latin composition; three books of Caesar's Gallic wars; four books of the *Aeneid* of Virgil, and six orations of Cicero;

3. Greek grammar and *Jacob's Greek Reader;*

4. Mathematics, including arithmetic, algebra, and three books of geometry (Davis's *Legendre*).

By 1890 the professors at the University of Alabama realized that the students from certain Alabama high schools seemed to do well consistently on their admission exams. They established the University Auxillary Schools in Alabama that they accredited and planned to admit their students by certificate. These schools included:

Marengo Military Academy, Demopolis
Verner Military Academy, Tuscaloosa
Livingston Military Academy, Livingston
University School , Montgomery
Greenville Public School, Greenville
Brundidge High School, Brundidge
University Military School, Mobile
South Highland Academy, Birmingham
Butler High School, Butler
State Normal College, Florence
Millwood School, Anniston
Snowden Academy, Snowden

The University of Alabama became a member of the Association of College and Preparatory Schools of the Southern States in 1897, and then adjusted its requirements to meet standards. The entrance exams were as follows:

1. English: Students were asked to write a paragraph on each of the following: The contest between Palamon and Arcite, the story of Alice Pyncheon, and "Sir Roger at the Theater."

2. Write a character sketch of Macbeth, give Carlyle's estimate of Burns as a poet, and write an outline of Milton's life from 1660 to1674 .

3. American History: Name the oldest city in the United States and tell when it was founded and by whom.

4. Discuss the beginning and the end of the Revolutionary War and include dates.

5. Give a sketch of the life of Andrew Jackson.

6. What led to the Compromise of 1850?

7. Give the four presidential tickets of 1860.

8. Give the dates that best describe the beginning and the end of the Civil War.

9. Name the capitals of the German Empire, the French Republic, and the Kingdom of Spain.

10. Name the two great rivers in India and where they flow.

11. Name the mountain range which bounds Italy on the north and the range that extends down the Italian peninsula.

12. Name the five great American states lying north of the

Ohio River and east of the Mississippi River.

13. Prove the following theorems in geometry. In addition,

there were questions of Latin, Greek, and algebra.

In 1871, there were issues that the overwhelming majority of Southern residents knew little about. For example, at the university there was no academic security for the faculty, which had to work with an inadequate salary and with the knowledge that their appointment was on a year-by-year basis. The university was a military school until the end of the century. Student life was restrained and controlled by the university. There were dances at the university for the students until the moralists in Tuscaloosa complained. At that point, the authorities outlawed all dances, which caused protests from the students. The administration finally relented and approved the following dances: The Grand March, Waltz, Polka, Mazourka, and the York.

Although the University of Alabama had the authority to admit women as students ten years before Oberlin College in 1833, it took the work of Julia Tutwiler to change things at this Southern university. In 1893, women were admitted to the University of Alabama.(20)

Chapter 7

Concluding Observations

It is obvious that the major difference between rebuilding after a natural disaster and a manmade catastrophe was the presence of strong and consistent leadership at Tulane University. Unfortunately for the University of Alabama, the challenge to rebuild the university was stalled in large part because of the Reconstruction period in the South. One of the best descriptions of life in the South immediately after the Civil War is given in the *State of Jones* by Sally Jenkins and John Stauffer.(13) Although this book centers on the misery and destruction that prevailed in the state of Mississippi after the Civil War, the situation throughout the South was similar, particularly in Alabama during those Reconstruction years.

Union soldiers, many of them black, occupied the South to enforce law and order. The locals visualized these soldiers as a reminder of their own defeat. The Old South was no longer in existence. Entire villages and towns had been destroyed. Food and potable water were scarce. There were few intact businesses, no jobs, no medications, no hospitals, and few doctors. Even the doctors who were around could do very little to help patients fight malaria, cholera, or yellow fever, all of which killed many people.

Even those Southerners who were considered affluent before the war were now paupers, just like the rest of the Southerners. Most everyone in the South had a family member or a neighbor who had been killed in the war or who had died of some disease, such as smallpox. It was a common sight to see men returning from the war missing an arm or leg. The farm fences were no longer standing, and there were no crops still growing that required harvesting. For many years after the war it was very common to see children eating clay. Some of the slave owners refused to allow their slaves to leave the farms, and only the intervention of the Union soldiers helped to separate the former slaves from their masters.

President Andrew Johnson still believed that the former Southern leaders should still be in control of the affairs in the South. The prevalent opinion among many white Southerners was that the "Negro" should not have any rights, and that it was not a crime to cheat Negroes, kill Negroes, or to sexually assault Negroes. Many felt that African Americans still belonged to the white Southerners. Since this was the prevailing attitude, one can see why it took years for the University of Alabama to recover. The governance of the University of Alabama was taken over by the Alabama State Legislature, until the Union soldiers left the state. Even if the state legislature had not been composed of carpetbaggers, scalawags, and freed slaves, there were so many other issues to resolve in the State of Alabama than the rebuilding of the University of Alabama.

Fortunately for Tulane University, the senior administrative leaders rose to the occasion under the leadership of President Scott Cowen, with the help of the Senior Vice President Yvette Jones and the Chief of Staff Anne Banos. Conceiving the Tulane Renewal Plan, and then executing that plan, sometimes over the objection of some members of the Tulane community, was a stroke of genius. The national visibility of the natural disaster and the subsequent rebuilding of New Orleans and Tulane University were covered in detail by the media.

After President Barack Obama's visit to New Orleans in late October 2009, Amy Liu of the Brookings Institute asked, "What will be the community's unified message about its progress and vision for the future?" How New Orleans and Tulane University respond to that question will shape the perceptions that others have of New Orleans and establish expectations about the city's future, according to President Scott Cowen in his editorial in the *Times-Picayune*, which appeared on www.nola.com/opinions October 24, 2009.(7) Cowen stated that not only is New Orleans embarking on a full recovery, but it also aspires to become "the model city for the twenty-first century." If Tulane and New Orleans are able to convert the tragedy into an opportunity and positive change, then they can say Hurricane Katrina made them stronger and better.

Finally, as this is being written, U.S. District Judge Stanwood R. Duval, Jr., ruled that in large part the destruction of New Orleans was due to negligence on the part of the Army Corps of Engineers in maintaining a shipping channel known as the Mississippi River Gulf Outlet. Because of this negligence a "hurricane highway" was created, which enabled flooding to occur in the eastern part of New Orleans and St. Bernard Parish. The judge awarded $720,000 in damages to four individuals and one business. Although the Army Corps of Engineers plans to appeal this decision, the door may now be opened for many more lawsuits to be filed in behalf of the citizens of New Orleans.

Notes

1. Douglas Brinkley, *The Great Deluge: Hurricane Katrina, New Orleans, and the Mississippi Gulf Coast* (New York: William Morrow, 2006).

2. Ray B. Browne and Lawrence A. Kreiser, Jr., *The Civil War and Reconstruction, American Popular Culture Through History* (Westport, Connecticut: Greenwood Press, 2003).

3. Richard Campanela, *Bienville's Dilemma: A Historical Geography of New Orleans* (Lafayette, Louisiana: Center for Louisiana Studies, University of Louisiana at Lafayette, 2008): 111–114.

4. Clark E. Center, "The Burning of the University of Alabama," *Alabama Heritage,* Issue no. 16 (1990): 30–45.

See also www.alabamaheritage.com/vault/UAburning. htm.

5. Clark E. Center, *Encyclopedia of Alabama*, September 12, 2008. See also http://encyclopediaofalabama.org/face/ Article Printable.jsp?id,6p

6. Willis G. Clark, "History of Education in Alabama, 1702–1889," Washington: Government Printing Office, 1889, 280 pages.

7. Scott S. Cowen, "Shaping Our Image Post-Katrina, a guest column by Scott S. Cowen. *The Times-Picayune* See also http://www.nola.com/opinions/index.ssf/2009/10/ shaping_ou,Oct.24,2009.

8. Scott S. Cowen, "My Day with President Obama," –An e-mail communication with all alumni via the Alumni affairs network.

9. J. G. Cowan, "The Destruction of the University of Alabama in April 1865," *Alabama University Bulletin*, (1901): 37–44.

10. John P. Dyer, *Tulane, The Biography of a University 1834–1965* (New York: Harper & Row, 1966).

11. Eugene Pieter Romayn Feldman, *Black Power in Old Alabama: The Life and Stirring Times of James T. Rapier, Afro-American Congressman from Alabama 1839–1883,* Museum of African American History, Chicago, Illinois, 1968.

12. Spencer S. Hsu, "Katrina Compensation Urged as Judge Faults Army Corps," *Washington Post*, 20 November 2009.

13. Sally Jenkins and John Stauffer, *The State of Jones—The Small Southern County that Seceded from the Confederacy* (New York: Doubleday, 2009), 231–280.

14. Samuel Will John, "Alabama Corps of Cadets 1860–65," *The Confederate Veteran* 25 (1917):12–14.

15. David G. Kline, "Inside and Somewhat Outside Charity," *Journal of Neurosurgery* 106, No. 1 (2007):180–188.

16. Ellen Condliffe Lagemann, *Education, Reader's Companion* 313–17 See Lawrence A. Cremin, *American Education: The National Experience, 1783–1876* (New York: Harper & Row, 1980).

17. Edward G. Longacre, ed., "To Tuscaloosa and Beyond: A Union Cavalry Raider in Alabama, March–April 1865," *The Alabama Historical Quarterly* 44, Spring & Summer (1982): 109–122.

18. Robert Mellown, "Tuscaloosa During the Civil War," *Historic Tuscaloosa—Essays & Guides*, http:// historictuscaloosa.org/civilwar.html.

19. Clarence L. Mohr and Joseph E. Gordon, *The Emergence of a Modern University, 1945-1980* (Baton Rouge, Louisiana: Louisiana State University, 2001).

20. James B. Sellers, *History of the University of Alabama* (Tuscaloosa, Alabama: University of Alabama Press, 1953): vol. 1, 1818–1902, 291–571.

21. *Tulane Renaissance* (Nashville, Tennessee: The Booksmith Group, 2007).

22. Suzanne Rau Wolfe, *The University of Alabama: A Pictorial History, The Military University 1860–1903* (Tuscaloosa, Alabama: University of Alabama Press, 1983) 60, 62, 82.